E. W.

KENYON'S
Living
Poems

WHITAKER
HOUSE

Kenyon's Living Poems

Kenyon's Gospel Publishing Society
P.O. Box 973
Lynnwood, WA 98046-0973
www.kenyons.org

ISBN: 978-1-64123-403-0
Printed in the United States of America
© 1998, 2020 by Kenyon's Gospel Publishing Society

Whitaker House
1030 Hunt Valley Circle
New Kensington, PA 15068
www.whitakerhouse.com

No part of this book may be reproduced or transmitted in any form or by any means, electronic or mechanical—including photocopying, recording, or by any information storage and retrieval system—without permission in writing from the publisher. Please direct your inquiries to permissionseditor@whitakerhouse.com.

This book has been printed digitally and produced in a standard specification in order to ensure its continuing availability.

These helpless little rhythms,
    That the printer here imprisons
Are not to blame,
    So you censors, please be mild
With my first poetic child—
    It's not to blame.

MY PRAYING FRIEND

I wandered once in sin's broad way,
    And siren songs I heard;
They led me on from day to day,
    Their voice my passions stirred;
They lured me deeper in their toils,
    Until they gained control,
I threw my manhood to the winds,
    The tempter had my soul.

My mother's prayers forgotten were,
    And home ties lost their pow'r,
Sin's seductions held me fast,
    I deeper sank each hour;
Fond scenes at times would come to me,
    And Mother's face appear
Amid my hours of revelry,
    That filled my heart with fear.

A friend I had who would not leave
    Me hopeless in my sin,
But followed me with mighty prayer,
    That God would take me in;
His prayers prevailed, my soul awoke,
    Conviction deep and strong
Shook my whole being to its depth,
    I saw my guilt and wrong.

I turned in weakness to the Lord,
    And took a sinner's place,
Then God thru Christ redeemed my soul
    And filled me with His Grace;
I stand tonight, but grace redeemed,
    A child of God so blest,

A praying friend had rescued me,
    My soul has found its rest.

FREEDOM

Freedom, my Father God,
    Freedom in Thee;
Bondage has been my part,
    I must be free.
Broken each vow I make,
    Lost is the ground I take,
Oh, for Thine own Name's sake,
    Now set me free.

Freedom, my Father God,
    Freedom in Thee;
Long, long has Satan ruled,
    Ruled over me.
Oft' have I tried in vain,
    Only to fail again,
Bondage gives bitter pain,
    Oh, set me free.

Freedom, my Father God,
    Was bought for me;
Freedom my soul shall have,
    I will be free.
Broken each bond tonight,
    Freedom is worth the fight;
His Name gives me the right,
    I will be free.

Freedom, my Father God,
    Freedom for me;
My heart with rapture sings,

At last I'm free.
Long have I prayed for this,
   Craved for this heavenly bliss,
Praises are not amiss,
   Thank God, I'm free.

UNPARDONABLE SINS

Are there *sins* God cannot pardon,
   Where Christ's blood cannot avail,
Where the tender voice of Jesus,
   As He pleads will only fail?

Are there sins without remission,
   In this world and that to come,
Sins that Calv'ry never reaches,
   And that spell the sinner's doom?

Yes, my friend, there is grave danger,
   You may forfeit God's free grace;
You may grieve the Spirit from you,
   And repentance find no place.

You may close your mind to reason,
   While your heart grows hard and cold,
And deny Him for a season,
   In your pride and lust for gold.

But with age the heart is hardened,
   And the will is slow to move,
While the mind with care is burdened,
   And the life fixed in its groove.

Chorus

Today if you hear his voice,
   O, harden not your heart;

Today then make your choice,
    E'er He from you depart.

THE GOD WHO DWELLS IN ME

The God who put our sin away
    The God of Calvary
The God who gives eternal life
    Is the God who dwells in me.

The God who raised dead Lazarus
    The God who stilled the sea,
The God who water turned to wine,
    Is the God who dwells in me.

The God who fed the multitude,
    Who made the blind to see,
The God who stilled the raging sea,
    Is the God who dwells in me.

The God who broke the bars of death
    Imprisoned men set free,
The God who bore our ills and pains
    Is the God who dwells in me.

Chorus

The God who dwells in me,
    The God who dwells in me,
The God who gives eternal life
    Is the God who dwells in me.

THE CALL

There's a call comes ringing
    From the throne of God,

To the men of every clime,
   To rise and fight
     For home and right,
To help in this critical time.

There's a call comes ringing
   From the heart of God,
To the men of every creed
   To rise and live
     Their best to give,
To meet humanity's great need.

There's a call comes ringing
   From the Word of God,
To the men: Give up your sin,
   And rise and be
     From bondage free,
In your souls great victories win.

There's a call comes ringing
   From the marts of gold,
For a man of might and power,
   To rise and lead,
     If need be, bleed,
For the world in its darkest hour.

HE DWELLS IN ME

He dwells in me,
He dwells in me,
The Mighty One now dwells in me,
He makes Himself reality
This Mighty One who lives in me.
   He dwells in me,
   He dwells in me,

The risen One now dwells in me,
His resurrection power gives me
This Risen One has set me free.
    He reigns in me,
        He reigns in me,
The Coming One now reigns in me,
The Lord of Life He is to me,
This Coming One will come for me.

SWEET SURRENDER

All that He is is mine today,
    With me Love's best He's sharing,
For Love has made Him one with me,
    For things He loves I'm caring.

I am what He says I am,
    To you this truth I'm telling,
He made me what I am Himself,
    My heart with Rapture's swelling.

My risen Lord makes me His home,
    His life in me He's living,
His best at last my heart has found,
    That best to me He's giving.

All that I am, His Love has made me,
    In me His life He's living,
Our wills at last in Him are one,
    To Him all praise I'm giving.

THE SECRET

My heart is full of laughter,
    My lips are full of song;

I'm praising God, my Father,
    The whole day long.

My life is full of sunshine,
    My soul is full of light;
There is joy in simple living,
    The world's so bright.

My days are full of gladness,
    My nights are full of joy;
While living in His presence,
    Trials don't annoy.

My work is only pleasure,
    My burdens light to bear;
While walking with the Father
    All days are fair.

I've felt the pangs of sorrow,
    I've known the night of pain;
With nothing in tomorrow
    To live was vain.

One night I met the Father,
    That night I learned to live;
My joy is not in getting,
    But in what I give.

THE SONG

I sat that night in a crowded hall,
    And heard the gospel sung;
It thrilled the heart of that mighty host,
    It swayed both old and young.

Yes, they sang the famous "Glory Song,"
    And "He Will Hold Me Fast";

The songs that have reached the world's great heart
    Songs that will ever last.

They sang of mother, home, and heaven,
    They sang of joys and love;
They sang of hope, of sins forgiven,
    Of Christ who reigns above.

And while they sang, I forgot the pain,
    Long hidden in my heart;
And lifting up my trembling voice,
    By grace I took my part.

Chorus

    Come, let us sing these songs of hope,
    And fill the world with light and love;
    Forget the toils, the pains and fears,
    And sing of our blest Home above.

MY CONFESSION

Through lips of clay He speaks today,
    His message clear and tender,
His living Word through men is heard,
    Our best in service render.

I am what He says I am,
    That is my glad confession;
I live in Him, He lives in me,
    Gone is my transgression.

What He says I can do, can be done,
    The Mighty One's indwelling,
His grace and wisdom both are mine,
    His wonders I am telling.

In me He lives, my gracious Lord,
    In me Himself is building,
His love law rules my life today,
    To Him my best I'm yielding.

His love law rules this heart of mine,
    We live in sweet communion,
My body now He makes His home
    Yes, this is heaven's union.

He is my Lord, my risen head,
    My mighty intercessor;
He died for me, He lives for me,
    With Him I'm joint possessor.

THE PROMISE

When God placed man in Eden,
    Amid the glories there,
He gave him full dominion,
    Put all beneath his care;
No curse rests on the garden,
    No sin nor pain was known,
Death had not cursed creation,
    Nor taught its lips to moan.

Then came the mighty tempter,
    Up from his dread domain,
To curse God's fair creation,
    Give birth to sin and pain;
The man yields to temptation,
    And filled with treason's blight,
He sells his vast possessions,
    Then all is plunged in night.

Man's driven from the garden,
    With no approach to God,
Save through bleeding sacrifice,
    Whose blood flows o'er the sod;
For man is dead in spirit,
    And Satan rules o'er him;
Then thru this cursed relation
    Man's sorrows reach the brim.

When driven out of Eden,
    By Justice's awful rod,
A promise then was given,
    Of Christ—Incarnate God,
Who'd break the rule of Satan,
    The claims of Justice pay,
Restore the lost Creation,
    Bring in Millennial Day.

THE OLD DAYS

There are no friends like the old friends,
    And no days like the days of old;
There are no hearts like the old hearts,
    So frank, so free, so bold,
And I want them again tonight.

There are no times like the old times,
    No joys like the joys of old;
There are no boys like the old boys,
    So true, so tried—pure gold,
And I want them again tonight.

There are no folks like the old folks,
    And no loves like the loves of old;
There are no girls like the old girls,

So fair, so sweet to hold,
And I want them again tonight.

There are no songs like the old songs,
    That we sang in the days of old;
There are no chums like the old chums—
    Can mem'ries e'er grow cold?
No, I want them again tonight.

Oh, give me back those days of old,
    When the heart was pure,
And my world was young;
    When my faith was sure,
And my song unsung,
    Oh, give me back those days of old.

MY LADDIE MINE

You're all that's left me, Laddie boy,
    Life's strip'd me to the bone,
Life's evening shadows now are near,
    You're going; I'm alone.
My name you bear, my Laddie dear,
    Life's dream heads up in you,
In you my last deposit's made,
    So if you fail, I'm thru.

But you won't fail—go win the game,
    Give life your best today;
Go make your best a better best
    You're at the bat! now play.
We'll win this game, I'll fight in you,
    They can't whip us, I know;
We two are one, so you count two,
    We're both behind each blow.

My dreams, my hopes, my faith's in you,
    You're my sole ambition;
So if you fail then I have failed,
    —Failed then, is my mission.
I don't know what in life you'll find,
    Or what they'll find in you,
But this I want for you my lad;
    A man, clean thru and thru.

For life is big when you join hands
    With Him the great Unseen—;
He'll walk with you, thru burning sands,
    In trials be your screen.
So fearless go as once I went,—
    A lad, I walked alone;
I walked the burning sands by faith,
    As you will when I'm gone.

THE BIRTH OF SONG

When music wedded poetry
    The muses laughed with glee,
They made the woods and valleys ring,
    With Love's own minstrelsy;
The muses planned to match these two,
    E're man first dreamed his dream,
Or music lay in Love's embrace,
    In rhythm's mystic stream.

Love asked the muses for a song,
    They sought for inspiration,
They traveled far, they traveled wide,
    Throughout the vast creation;
By chance they spied a maiden's heart,

In holy meditation,
Then at the fount, they knelt, they drank,
    In quiet expectation.

There born was song—that sacred thing,
    To gladden all creation,
It caused the birds to pipe and sing,
    In wildest jubilation;
The flowers caught the spirit too,
    Poured forth in glad profusion,
The perfume from their golden hearts,
    In dainty sweet effusion.

Then glad it made the heart of man,
    This mystic art of muses
That gathers from the heart of love,
    The cure for all its bruises;
It searches deep the realm of love,
    Its treasures rich revealing,
It scans the very throne of God,
    Then sings with Love's appealing.

MY BOAT

My little boat floats o'er the foam,
    A dainty craft is she,
To foreign lands she loves to roam,
    She e'er returns to me.

My little boat's a fairy craft,
    She does not fear the sea,
In many climes, she casts her lines,
    Her merchandise brings me.

My little boat's a wayward boat,
    Much trouble causes me,
She goes at night, quite out of sight,
    Upon a stranger sea.

But she'll return with tears that burn
    The very heart of me,
She can but live, if I forgive,
    That's what she whispers me.

My wayward boat, that fain will float,
    Upon some stranger sea,
The load she bore, was hearts a score,
    And yet, she sails for me.

My fragile boat, on seas remote,
    Sails happy, proud and free,
Yes, she'll return, my love won't spurn,
    She says, she loves but me.

My dainty boat, I'll have you note,
    Is true as truth can be,
And yet I fear, when she's not near,
    She's swallowed by the sea.

I dreamed tonight, that all's not right,
    My heart can breakers see,
And now I fear, the truth to hear,
    That she is lost to me,

Her anchor's cast, a broken mast,
    She sails no more for me,
Her sail is furled, I've lost my world,
    She's dead upon the sea.

A SYMPHONY OF MEMORY

'Twas mem'ry's silent symphony
That held me quiet there—
'Twas Love's own holy rhapsody
That floated on the air.
A tune that stole up mem'ry's lane,
Where lovers walked of yore;
Had tears mixed in its melody,
Like singing just offshore.
The halting rhythm in the tune
Its dainty undertone,
Had stripped away the broken years,
And left me there alone.
For mem'ries have their melodies,
As songs are born in tune;
And heartaches have their litanies,
In December as in June.

LOVE WORDS

Wise was he who coined love words,
Wiser he who used no other,
Glad was he who heard the love words
Gladder that he'd found a brother.

LOVE'S MINSTREL

Love's minstrel long had silent been,
    Its bow disused, unstrung,
        The muses, silent, sat apace,
            Love's dream was still unsung.

The muses stirred expectantly,
    They struck Love's ancient lyre,

Then Love awoke, the magic stroke
Had set her soul afire.

At first her voice refused to sing
This song, so new, so thrilling;
Her strength was gone, she feared the song
That all her soul was willing.

Her fears dissolved in ecstasy,
Her being caught the fire,
She rose, enwrapt in Love's white flame,
And clasped the ancient lyre.

She struck the strings and Love leaped forth,
Love's lambent flame eternal,
And passion answered Love's refrain
In melody supernal.

Then deep she drank at Love's fair fount,
But ne'er her thirst assuages,
For fires that burn in Love's glad urn
Will thirst thru all the ages.

PAIN'S PEARLS

We wait the muse's inspiration,
The touch of her magic wand,
The thrill of her divination,
A view of enchanted land.

She guides in paths of mystery
Where our feet have never trod,
She fills the air with melody
As she waves the mystic rod.

The Delphic lamp of mystic light
Now illumes our pathway drear,

And drives the darkness into night
And dries the gathering tear.

The muses have learned the secret
Of turning our tears to pearls,
And midnight pain to daylight gain;
Then our faith its flag unfurls.

THORN-CROWNED

The thorn-scarred brow of the Man of Galilee,
Revealed a love that was new to me,
A love so strange to this selfish age,
It never was dreamed by priest or sage,
A love that died, that others might live,
A love, that all gave, that He, all might give.
That Love was a standard of a new race of men.
That was to rise from the grave of that lone Galilean,
That race was to be known as the twice-born men,
Who live in Love's realm, beyond reason's ken,
That new race of men, by Faith were to talk.
You know of their presence by their love-ruled walk.

CAPTIVE MELODY

A melody came floating by,
    Dainty as zephyr's wing,
Filled with a fleeting harmony,
    For angels fit to sing.

The melody was caught that day,
    Like nectar from a rose,
Imprisoned on a paper white,
    Which bars and notes impose.

The melody was freed that night,
    Cast forth upon the air
From the trembling strings of a violin,
    Played by a maiden fair.

The melody was caught again!
    A poet heard the tune
The words came bursting from his heart
    To wed that wandering rune.

The melody and words were wed,
    Both blended in the tune,
And happy were they from that day
    As couples wed in June.

AT LAST

The muses will gather, in conclave tonight
To settle the question if Love has the right
To confuse a man's mind, entangle his heart,
To make him Love blind, and then call that art?
The muses that gather in conclave, my friend,
Will solve that whole problem, and bring to an end,
That despotic rule of the heart's mighty queen,
Man they'll set free! If a maid, don't intervene?

THE DEEP, DEEP WOODS

I get so tired of people
    And long for solitude,
Where tall pine trees are sighing,
    That ev'ry care exclude.

Oh, I get so tired of people,
    Their jealousies and pride,

I long for holy solitude,
    In deep woods far to hide.

The heaping up of treasure,
    The eternal thirst for gold,
The cruelties of leisure,
    Where virtue's bought and sold.

Oh, the cities banish beauty,
    The pavements rob of rest,
While multitudes are tiresome
    The deep woods are the best.

The lust of gold's a canker,
    The pride of life's a bane,
The price we pay for pleasure
    Is virtue's deathless pain.

How homeless are their mansions,
    How restless are their beds,
How comfortless their millions,
    How tired their scheming heads.

What a price they pay for pleasure
    That leaves a bleeding heart,
And how joyless is their leisure,
    How bitter is the smart.

Just give me the open country
    With God's clear blue above,
With dainty flowers for company,
    All nature making love.

Then this heart of mine is happy,
    I'm richer than a king,
The laughing of the rivulet
    While birds and insects sing.

You may have your city pleasures,
    Dance and the opera too,
Give me God's great cathedral,
    'Mid pines and cedars true.

LONELINESS

I know what it means to be lonely,
In the midst of a multitude,
And to feel the depths of loneliness,
In a noisy solitude.

I know what it means to be lonely,
In a gay and thoughtless crowd;
When the lone heart cries for fellowship,
And no fellowship's allowed.

I know what it means to be lonely,
When words their meaning have lost;
When the speech of a friend is prattle—
The heart's stopped counting the cost.

I know what it means to be lonely—
The heart lives in solitude,
With silence vast as the blue above—
Naught can that silence intrude.

OLD AGE CONSCIOUS

I didn't think old age would come
And find me unprepared;
It stole upon me unawares,
And here I am white haired.

I have not done the work I'd planned,
In fact I've just began
To find my place in life's great scheme,
And now I've run the span.

I cannot stop—I must go on,
Time must yield me a place,
Where I can do this stint of mine,
Ere I have run my race.

THE FIRST SNOW

Dainty snowflakes softly falling,
For the sleigh bells gently calling,
Tho' they swiftly change to rain,
They persist and come again;
Little children love the snow,
This the snowflakes seem to know,
So they're falling all around,
On the streets all o'er the town;
Hear the children laugh in glee,
At the snowflakes we all see,
Soft and silent tho' they fall,
You can't count them one and all;
Soon they'll cover all the land,
And drift knee deep where you stand
Dainty snowflakes softly falling,
For the sleigh bells they are calling
Calling, calling, gently calling
For the sleigh bells they are calling.

MELODY OF MISERY

The melody of anguish,
    Is in the minor key,
The sighs and tears of broken hearts,
    Are love's own litany.

The hunger cry of masses
    Is the melody of pain,
A symphony of broken dreams,
    Set to a minor strain.

The slaves of want and misery,
    Never sing in a major key,
Their songs are full of discord wild,
    And broken harmony.

The melody of broken lives,
    The funeral dirge of dreams,
Bitter lyric and hopelessness,
    In passion's turgid streams.

THAT PERFECT ME

That trouble's never in myself
    It's always in the other
I seldom quarrel with myself
    It's with my little brother.

If you my way would always give
    And my will would never cross
With me you'd find it nice to live
    I would love to be your boss.

CONTENTMENT

A mind content is wealth untold,
It makes the spirit free and bold,
With just enough the need to meet,
Each morning sun with joy they greet.

If they had more, more they would grieve,
In fearing some their horde would thieve,
By being poor, they're rich they find,
With hordes of sweet content of mind.

They have their garden and their flowers,
They have their early morning hours,
They have their work, they have their play,
They have contentment all the day.

They envy not the idle rich,
Content they are in their own niche,
To buy and sell, to give and save,
To little have and little crave.

They are content, yes, this is life,
Without ambition's bitter strife,
The neighbor's wealth they covet not,
His goods are safe from hidden plot.

Their end is sweet, a quiet rest,
They found in life God's very best,
They fear not God when Him they meet,
A happy child, their Father greet.

LIFE'S MELODIES

There are raptures meet for music,
    That no master hand could play,

There are melodies so subtle,
    That in silence fade away;
There are chords of deepest anguish,
    To the broken heart belong,
There are rests of solemn silence,
    That have found no place in song.

There are bursts of heav'nly anthems,
    And the dirge of earthly pain,
There's the minor of the death song,
    And the warrior's martial strain
There's the lover's ardent carol,
    And the mother's lullaby,
There's the toiler's holy night song,
    And the outcast's bitter cry.

There are children's happy spring songs,
    And the mother's lonely wail,
There's the matron's quiet matin,
    And the maiden's holy grail;
There are songs of hope 'mid trials,
    And the songs of deep despair,
There's the melody of mis'ry,
    With the pain that has no tear.

There's the melody of silence,
    While it suffers deepest wrong,
There's the harmony of anguish,
    To the sweetest joys belong;
Our tenderest songs have birth pangs,
    Our holiest hours give pain,
Our loftiest songs, confessions,
    And life sacrifice is gain.

OUR NATIONAL DREAM

Our national dream's a golden dream,
    We see and dream but yellow,
E'en the sun's warm gleam's a golden beam,
    Like leaves in autumn mellow.

Our national flow'r's the Goldenrod,
    A fitting emblem, you'll say,
For those who worship the golden god,
    Whose hearts on its altar lay.

Our national god's a golden god,
    In this god of gold we trust,
For Him we bleed, in our wanton greed,
    Our god of the golden lust.

Our national sin's a golden sin,
    We sin in a royal way,
We're big and strong, in our golden wrong,
    "Then let the orchestra play."

Our national game's the golden game,
    In riots gamble golden
Our god and home, or the Capitol's dome,
    From it, we're not withholden.

Our national law's the golden law,
    That rules the House and Senate,
Our trusts are bold, in their rule of gold,
    With hellish lust incarnate.

If our nation's heart had golden blood,
    We'd coin it into dollars,
Yes, bleed her dry, and let her die,
    And wear foul slavery's collars.

Man thinks in terms of gold today,
    Genius is rated by ems,
All that's holy is sold today,
    Virtue is bartered for gems.

OUR GOLDEN CRIME

Our nation's dream is a golden stream,
    That flows thru our marts today,
Our men are bold in their quest for gold,
    And naught can their passion stay.

Our nation's crime is the golden slime,
    That defiles our homes today;
Our hellish greed makes the poor man bleed,
    The bills our children will pay.

Our nation's pride is the golden bride,
    They woo on our street of shame,
To our nation's grief, they laud the thief,
    Who wins in the golden game.

Our nation's shame is this golden game,
    We play with the children's food,
Their hunger pain is our chance for gain,
    We're coining their tears and blood.

Our nation's lust is the golden trust,
    That's crushing our first ideal,
For a heap of gold, our dreams we've sold—
    And truth has lost her appeal.

Is there relief, from this golden grief,
    That poisons our nation's heart:
Will this curse of gold, cause moral mold—
    Truth from our nation depart?

Our dollar is stamped, "In God we trust,"
    The god we worship's well known,
It's the unclean god, of golden lust,
    For the true God's lost His throne.

Must the great God leave our nation?
    He left the nations of old!
Must the great God leave His people,
    Because they're worshiping gold?

THE GOLDEN RULE

I've a Golden Rule, and that rule, you see,
Is to do every one before he does me:
I'm out in the fight for dollars, you know,
And I work everyone who gives me a show.

I'll do him up brown if he's plenty green,
And show him some tricks he has never seen,
I'm honest and straight in business, you see,
I simply do others before they do me.

This Golden Rule is our rule to get gold,
And here's the reason so many get sold,
They're out in the fight but don't know the rule,
They ne'er studied in the Streets Sunday School.

This rule is well worked in both church and state,
They're working it too, both early and late,
They'd make all our laws to help the poor rich,
Who've caught that microbe, the dread golden itch.

This rule to get gold and to get it quick,
Raising the mischief with some of the slick,
They're numbered, alas, among fallen stars,
Who direct their business behind the bars.

Uncle Sam has heard of this rule of gold,
Has caused a stir and some feet to grow cold,
There's trouble today in the quick-rich crowd,
They're howling at Sammy, both long and loud.

They're spoiling this land of the golden fleece,
That meddlesome bunch! Will they ever cease?
We'll never get rich if the people get wise—
That the good endure it, to me's a surprise.

MY NURSE'S FIGHT

Silent like an angel moving
    'Round the death bed, tender, loving,
        Patient, watchful, ever heeding
        Any comfort that is needing—
    Silent,
        Strong.

Fiercely burns the fiery fever,
    Delirium grips and will not leave her,
        Pulse and breath are playing faster,
            On the edge of hope's disaster—
    She—
        Fights on.

With grim Death, at last she's fighting,
    Nature's balance knows no righting,
        Here, no quarter's ever given,
            To the last ditch see her driven,
    Fighting—
        Fine.

Nurse and doctor's eyes are meeting,
    Both intent on Death defeating,

  She's defiant, no retreating
    While there's life and pulse is beating,
     She—
      Is game.

Death, in ambush, nearer gliding,
  At the heart his arrows guiding,
    All the night his time was biding,
     Now he comes, has left his hiding—
      She
       Can't yield.

Death's cold hand the pulse is gripping,
  Life is waning—hold is slipping,
    Light is fading—spirit's leaving—
     Death is winning!—stops! the breathing—
      Has—
       She lost?

THE FAILURE

I have drunk the wine of failure,
  Been drunken thru and thru,
Have worn old clothes that did not fit,
  When every flower was blue.

I have feared to face the mailman,
  For I knew the mail was bills,
That every letter had a dun,
  I know life's bitter chills.

I know this world of heartaches,
  I know this world of ills,
I know the fight for simple life,
  I know the rents and bills.

I know the smiling salesman,
    I know the collector's frown,
I know the promise of success,
    And the promise broken down.

I know of hopes with rosy hues,
    I know of deep despair,
I know the rainbow after storm—
    No gold awaits me there.

I know ambition's holy glow,
    And failure's biting pain,
I know the truth when script to skin,
    And every hope is slain.

I know when time has done its work,
    And chances all are past,
And dim eyes wistful backward turn,
    The heart's torn flag's half-mast.

God will not leave us broken there,
    In failure's deadly gloom,
But mend our wrecked and shattered faith,
    Once more, life's hope will bloom.

SECRET OF SUCCESS

Success was so illusive
    I've tried her oft in vain,
Yet she was so effusive,
    I thought I'd try again.

She smiled and beckoned to me
    It seemed a dead sure hit,
I borrowed all the cash I could,
    O friends, that's how I bit.

The other fellow had my cash,
  I had wisdom bitter,
I swore I'd never bite again,
  However bright the glitter.

I tried my hand at poetry
  It never reached the press,
Then I tried to save the world,
  From industrial distress.

I wrote a dozen essays
  Which the public wouldn't read,
I tried my hand at novels
  The public paid no heed.

I went to raising chickens
  But they simply wouldn't hatch,
The grocer raised the dickens,
  And threatened to attach.

I turned me to psychology
  And taught how to succeed,
The wonder, friends, of wonders
  They all my books will read.

So friends, I found my level,
  It's giving folks advice
And strange they all will take it,
  And pay me my own price.

MY FRIENDS

True friends are rare,
  I know but few:
    Chief of them all
      I reckon you.

Strange years are they,
    Since first I knew
        The soul's safe rest,
            In friends like you.

Your friendship pure,
    Like mountain dew,
        Has strengthened me,
            These long years through.

I look tonight
    At coming years,
        To share with you,
            My joys and tears.

I can't afford
    And how can you,
        To lose a friend,
            Whose heart rings true?

I need your love,
    And you need mine,
        For friendship's love,
            Is strong and fine.

Come, let us now
    A moment spend,
        To keep the one
            We count as friend.

For days will come,
    When friends are few,
        And you need me,
            And I need you.

FRIENDS

My friends are few,
    But very rare:
        To me they're true,
            That's all I care.

In summer sun
    Or winter's snow,
        They swear by me,
           How e'er it blow.

We borrow some,
    To some we lend:
        We keep no books,
           We trust a friend.

We may not meet
    The whole year thru;
        We keep in touch—
           What else we do.

For friends are rare,
    And friends are few,
        And better are
           The old than new.

Old friends will fight
    When new ones run:
        They stand by you
           In fuss or fun.

So let us keep
    The friends, tho' few
        Who've stood the test,
           These long years thru.

THE FEAR OF OLD AGE

A thousand fears assail my heart,
    As old age comes apace,
I've counted every pain and ache
    Each line upon my face.

I've watched the brown hairs silver turn,
    The change in face and form,
The growing fear of poverty,
    I face life's final storm.

My youthful dreams are faded now,
    The love of conquest past,
A quiet country home for me,
    Life's flag is now half-mast.

I dream no more of fortunes vast,
    Or conquest o'er the sea,
My little world has narrow grown,
    A cottage now, for me.

I watch youth's fond ambitions now,
    With a kindly wistful smile,
I've had my dream, I've had my day,
    I'm on life's last half-mile.

I do not fear life's fading light,
    The dread of age has flown,
While quiet faith its place has filled,
    Love's joy has fears outgrown.

HOW MEN FIGHT

When the burdens are too heavy,
    And your faith has lost its grip,

And the trials are so many,
    That you fear the brakes will slip:
Draw your belt a little tighter,
    Straighten up a wee bit more,
Sing a snatch of some old faith song,
    Strike out boldly from the shore.

What you need is room and current,
    And deep water for your boat,
For you're loaded to the gunwales,
    But the old thing sure will float;
Face the issue, don't get rattled,
    Think your problem thru and thru,
Take a chance but never gamble,
    To your friends ring clean and true.

For this fight is not for weaklings,
    But for men who stand the gaff,
Who can face life's changing problems,
    And meet failure with a laugh;
Few men win in life's hard struggle,
    Who have not been battle-scarred,
And their early dreams and castles,
    Have, alas, been sadly marred.

If you have not made your fortune,
    And gray hairs your brow has crowned,
Now's the time to keep your courage,
    Tho' the fates on you have frowned;
Trust in God and in the people,
    Keep your faith tho' all goes wrong,
In the end, you're sure to triumph,
    For to that crowd you belong.

FAITH IN MY FAITH

Faith in my faith, that I'll stand true,
    Tho' waves are breaking o'er the deck,
When every rosy hope turns blue,
    And all life's plans a hopeless wreck,
That I'll stand true, that I'll stand true.

Faith in my faith, that I'll stand fast,
    And face myself, tho' all have fled,
Yes, look upon life's broken mast,
    Tho' every hope and dream are dead,
True to the last, true to the last.

Faith in my faith, tho' all should doubt,
    I'll take life's broken reed again,
And drive my every fear to rout,
    And sing my song of hope through pain,
That I'll win out, that I'll win out.

Faith in my faith, that I can't fail,
    While linked to God, I stand secure,
I'll face the storm with shattered sail,
    The prize he wins, who will endure,
And use the gale, and use the gale.

Refrain

Faith in my faith, that I will ever be,
    True to His faith, that He's reposed in me
Faith in His faith, that me He'll ever hold,
    True to His truth, what e'er that truth enfold.

WE TWO

Not passive love, nor fighting love,
    Not even dainty nagging,
Not finding fault, or quick assault;
    Nor little thoughtless lagging.

A love-poised mind, to some things blind
    E'er ready with forgiving,
The gentle smile, that cares beguile,
    Which makes life rich with living.

With kindly wit, slights to forget,
    Not even softly chiding,
Quick to defend, slow to offend,
    Hurt feelings always hiding.

To give and take,—hold firm the break,
    While down love way you're gliding
In love to live, your best to give,
    While o'er rough places riding.

Love's way is best, on this you rest,
    Love cannot lead you straying,
Love can't do wrong, Love makes you strong,
    Love all the bills is paying.

So down love way, they walk today,
    Their spirit love is blending,
They two are one, love's work is done,
    And joy they've found unending.

THE LURE OF GOLD

Life is losing its poetry,
    Love is losing its hold,

Lust is gaining supremacy,
    All thru the lure of gold.

Law is losing its dignity,
    And sin is growing bold,
Justice smiles at iniquity,
    All thru the lure of gold.

Church is losing its sanctity,
    Faith is losing its hold,
Wrong is gaining the mastery,
    All thru the lure of gold.

Man is losing his chastity,
    Virtue is being sold,
Marriage is but a travesty,
    All for the lure of gold.

Home is losing authority,
    Its priceless treasures sold,
In the marts of worldly pleasures,
    All for the lure of gold.

Man lives in the realm of gold today,
    It glitters in his eye,
He's leaving faith's glad fold today,
    For doubt's dark, low'ring sky.

Man thinks in terms of gold today,
    Genius is rated by ems,
All that's holy is sold today,
    Virtue is bartered for gems.

Will the great God leave His people,
    Since man has left His fold,
Will the great God leave His temple,
    Because they worship gold?

THE WORD

No Word from God, of power is void,
No idle Word He's spoken
In every sentence now He lives
His promise can't be broken.

A part is He, of all He's said
In every Word He's hidden
The Scriptures are one with Himself
To feast on it we're bidden.

The very life of God indwells
This Word, which He has given
The living Word, He now makes real
His Word that's fresh from heaven.

Chorus

O'er His Word the Lord is watching
And that Word He will perform
On this Word my heart is resting
While I stand amid the storm.

FIND YOUR PLACE

No one will fail, along life's trail,
    If their place they find,
They fail because they break the laws,
    Try to go it blind.

For one and all, there is a call,
    Talents always giv'n,
Success awaits, she ope's the gates,
    Into joy's haven.

So find your place, and hit the pace,
    Give to it your best,
And that best train, yes make it reign,
    And you will be blest.

YOU SLEW IT

Love's blood is on your hands, dear,
The mark you bear of Cain
The tear wet sod cries up to God,
Where you, dear love, have slain.

You slew it not as men slay men,
With bludgeon, or with lead,
You slew it, dear, with cruel jeer,
You left it there half dead.

The very lips that gave it life,
Those same lips gave death,
Those very lips with passion tipped
Have now a poisoned breath.

Your words of love, that love sustained,
Your words of hate now slay it,
That heart once fed on words you said,
Your words of hate betray it.

You could not miss, the stolen kiss,
Your lips were burning seeking,
Now those same lips, deep venom sips,
With hatred deep are reeking.

COMPLETE IN HIM

Complete in Him,
What grace divine,
Complete in Him,
What joy is mine—
Complete in Him,
'Tis all of grace,
In Him I've found
My hiding place.

Complete in Him,
What love! What grace,
In Him I've found,
My hiding place.
Complete in Him!
What love divine,
This life from God,
At last is mine.

HAS EVERY MAN A PRICE

"Has every man a price, my friend?"
    Is the question from of old;
Will all our nation's manhood bend,
    To the subtle pow'r of gold?

Is honesty an ideal friend
    That's cherished thru our land;
Do people need a mortgage, friend,
    If once we pledged our hand?

The man who sells his suffrage,
    That sacred right to vote,
Leaves nothing holy to defend,
    Nor manhood 'neath his coat.

When man will break his given word,
    Will barter it for gold;
His right to vote, he forfeits then
    Or suffrage rights to hold.

When man will sell his blood-bought rights
    For gold or fleeting fame,

Mark well his end, the curse will send,
    The burning blight of shame.

Who would his fellowman corrupt,
    To pave his way to fame,
Should spend his last days in a cell,
    In solitude and shame.

"Has every man a price, my friend?"
    I answered proudly, "No!"
We have some heroes of the truth,
    Who fear the traitor's woe.

AS MUCH AS GOLD

In the world where self is reigning,
    And the heart grows hard and cold,
Is there anything in living,
    That is worth as much as gold?

When the heart has lost its mooring,
    And the faith has lost its hold,
Is there anything in living,
    That is worth as much as gold?

When the life has lost ambition,
    And its heart dreams turn to mold,
Is there anything in living,
    That is worth as much as gold?

When the will's life blood is ebbing,
    And its final struggle's told,
Is there anything in living,
    That is worth as much as gold?

When the homes ties all are broken,
    And the last heart treasure sold,

Is there anything in living,
    That is worth as much as gold?

When the last farewell is spoken,
    And the winding sheet enfold,
Was there anything in living,
    That was worth as much as gold?

When the Lord we meet in judgment,
    And life's failure we behold,
We shall find there's much in living,
    That is worth far more than gold.

WHAT SHALL HE SING

Shall he sing to please the masses;
    Shall he sing to please his God;
Shall he sing to the inner circle,
    Or bear the divining rod?

Shall his voice be simply charming
    In a rhythmic cadence sweet,
With a message for the moment,
    For the thoughtless to repeat?

Should his voice be deadly earnest;
    Should his song crash on the ear,
With a warning cry of danger,
    Wake a slumbering nation's fear?

Should his song be strong and rugged,
    As a man speaks to a man,
With an honest love that's fearless,
    Dares a nation's sin to scan?

Should he tell them all white-heated
    With a soul that's set aflame,

Of the traitors of the nation,
    That now use us in their game?

Should he sacrifice his future
    In his almost mad desire,
To arouse a blinded people
    And awake their righteous ire?

Yes, thou lone but fearless singer,
    Lift your song against their sin,
And arouse their sleeping conscience
    'Till the light of truth shines in.

Your reward will be their curses,
    And your name they'll speak with hate.
But you'll save the nation's honor,
    Tho' they honor you too late.

God's true singer sings but solos,
    None with him a part will take;
He is singing for the ages,
    Tho' his own does not awake

FAITH'S VICTORY

Undaunted he stands amid the wreck
Of a life work wrought thru pain,
He cannot yield, or give the field,
Where doubt and fear would reign.

Faith cannot fail, it must prevail,
He meets loss with a smile,
Disaster's sneer, gives him no fear,
Faith holds the wheel the while.

He has not failed, until he yields
To doubt and maddening fear;

To these he will not trust the ship,
Faith knows success is near.

You cannot conquer faith, my friend,
With failure's bludgeon strong;
Faith rises victor over fear,
In triumph sings its song.

Faith cannot fail, it knows not how;
It never learned defeat;
It always fellowshipped success;
It's resting at her feet.

LOVE'S LAST LAMENT

All his life his heart was seeking,
    For its mate,
All thru youth its vigil keeping,
Disappointment ever meeting,
Hopes renewed, each morning greeting,
    Wooing fate.

Manhood's prime at last attending,
    Still no mate,
Passion blind the mount ascending,
Leashed by will, commands contending,
All his forces poised and blending,
    Held abate.

Years like tides pass by unheeding,
    Seeks his mate,
Fires of youth are now receding,
Some are banked, half draft is feeding,
On the fuel, age is needing,
    Yet no mate.

Cruel time his strength is biting,
        Needs a mate,
With old age at last he's fighting,
Chances lost, there is no righting,
Hopeless age—his heart is blighting,
        It's too late.

Oh, the pierced heart that's bleeding,
        For a mate,
For the gentle wife-touch pleading,
And her counsels ever needing,
On their face 'tis writ for reading—
        It is fate?

THE LOVE SLAVE'S SONG

My heart is Thine, come fill it Lord
    With love fresh from Thine own,
And tune it to Thine own high will,
    Yes, make this heart Thy throne;

My mind is Thine, I give it now,
    Come, think Thy thoughts thru me,
O live again in me dear Lord
    As in old Galilee.

My body's Thine, a temple make,
    Come live dear Lord in me,
Reveal Thyself, Thy very self,
    In rich reality;

These ears and hands, these eyes and feet,
    These lips to sing or pray;
My every faculty is Thine,
    To serve in Thine own way.

I've given all, now all is Thine,
    To use or lay aside,
My soul's content, I ask no more
    But in Thy will abide,

Here rest I find—yes, perfect rest,
    Thy will is sweet to me.
Thy will is mine, Thy joy is mine,
    My Lord's reality.

Chorus

I've willed my will to Thee dear Lord,
    This is the heart of all,
I have no more to give or hold,
    My best is at Thy call.

REGRETS WERE VAIN

No one is blamed—I did not inspire
Love in her breast,
I saw not love, but kindness and
Respect in her eyes
I looked for love, I looked in vain
I saw not love, but pitying pain,
And I passed on.

I saw the eyes kindle, the bosoms
Rise in sudden ecstasy
But it was for another
I heard the eager tones—the
Lover's tones of passion—
But it was not for me.

I went out into the barren night
Tho' it was yet the day to others

Cold dismal night fell on my soul—
No sun ever shines where I went
I wish her joy—him glad hours—
But it was cold for me
Cold, dark, and so alone
No light, no heat, just
Cold damp dreariness.

Years passed—again I saw her
She was sitting by the sea
She looked so weary—no rest
Could rest her
No quiet, could quiet that restless
Sea in her heart—
In her eyes I saw the mystery
That veils agony—
The silence that deep pain imparts—
I dare not intrude—
Mine were lost joys—I'd never explored;
Hers—were slain—brutally murdered joys
With no funeral—with no flowers—
Killed in her own deep heart.

I saw the death stroke in her face
I heard her speak—her voice had
The minor tones—melody of misery—
What melodies could be gleaned from
Desolate hearts;
I wandered on—wondered if the golden glow of love
Could ever light those eyes again—
If the pulses could thrill at the sound of a footfall,
If the bosoms ever sing the mating song again.

MIGHT IS RIGHT

I want to believe that justice and truth
    Are ruling men's hearts today,
That righteousness reigns in the marts of gold
    And that right and truth hold sway.

I know it's not true in the realm of gold,
    Might reigns as king of the street,
For might is right, in the business world,
    While truth lies bound at its feet.

For might is right in the realm of the strong,
    You've read in it prose, you've heard it in song,
Success makes you right, but failures are wrong,
    So He has no place in that gold-mad throng.

The means that they use, success justified,
    The truth and the masses were crucified;
The children may cry in their hunger pains,
    The street smiles broadly and counts its gains.

In the realm of self, old greed reigns as king,
    The weak have no place in the game,
They're simply chattel, slaughtered as cattle,
    But they pay the bills just the same.

The creed of success is the creed of the street
    To succeed is the dream of the hour,
To fail is a crime, in success's upward climb
    Fail to reach gold's enchanted bower.

THE SEEKER

In the mystic word of sages
That has come down thru the ages

I am seeking for the right
It's the light of human reason
That has oft committed treason
   In this struggle up to light.

But I trust these mystic sages
Who have left us cryptic pages
   That are hard to understand
For they have claimed the Delphic light
And many times the "second sight"
   And I follow their command.

For in their cryptic runes I find
There is no calm, for this poor mind
   So I'm searching, searching yet
In anguish for the muse I call
That master muse who rules us all
   For the light I cannot get.

Now I fear I doubt the sages
And their fatalistic pages
   But where shall I turn for light
For reason has no light divine
I cannot linger at her shrine
   Here is reason's bitter night.

LIFE AS IT IS

The misery of the age I taste,
   My mouth 'tis mother of gall,
Anguish and pain with agony,
   The unwanted lot of all.

Light is dim where we walk alone,
   Tho' a crowd is by our side,

For anguish makes each one, a one,
    And failure is each man's bride.

The optimist's not walking here,
    Where life is stript to the skin,
Theories can't face realities,
    Where every sole's worn thin.

Alone can love survive this test,—
    Faith's strong shield is broken
The light of hope is faded, gone!
    Dry grief is failure's token.

Better seems death than failure's shroud
    But we can't hide in the tomb,
Tho' light be dim, the fight must win
    And be the winner's groom.

THE ROYALTY OF SERVICE

There's a royalty in service,
    That the heart gives to its King,
When it yields its every treasure,
    And with joy these treasures bring—
To the object of its worship—
    With a heart too full to sing.

There's a royalty in service,
    When His grace reigns in the heart,
Turning duty into pleasure,
    Makes Love's ministry an art—
That will glorify our labors,
    And life's deepest joys impart.

There's a royalty in service,
    When the heart with love o'er flows,

That will welcome sacrifices,
    That no limit ever knows;
While the fragrance of their service,
    Is far sweeter than the rose.

Chorus

I'll serve my Lord, in love's royal way,
    My best I lay at His feet,
I'll give that best, in a royal way,
    His best, with my best, I'll meet.

MY GIFT

All my life I have yielded,
All upon the altar lay,
All the members of my body,
I have given all today.

All my talents I have given,
All upon the altar lay,
To be used in Thy blest service,
I have given all today.

All my money I have offered,
All upon the altar lay,
To be spent now for Thy kingdom,
I have given all today.

All my heart life I have yielded,
All its treasures are Thine own,
All my hopes and fond ambitions,
All are Thine, Thine alone.

Chorus

Oh, the joy of love's surrender,
Wondrous bliss! a yielded will;
All my being now responding,
Come, dear Lord, Thy temple fill.

HOW I FOUND HIM

When I had found all efforts fail,
Man's rarest gifts of no avail,
    Then I sought Him,
When boastful science left the field,
I faced defeat with shattered shield,
    Then I sought Him.

When I all other helps forsook,
And trusted only in that Book,
    Then God met me,
When I all other helps denied,
And trusted in the crucified,
    Then God met me,

'Twas when I sought with all my heart
Forsaking every human art,
    That I found Him,
In love He held me to his breast,
And I had found life's perfect rest,
    When I found Him.

When God they saw upholding me,
My failure turn to victory,
    They wanted Him,
And then they sought God's own success,
They found that He alone could bless,
    They too found Him

IN HIS ARMS

I have found a sure retreat,
    In His arms, in His arms,
I am near the mercy seat,
    In His arms, in His arms.

O how safe I'm resting here,
    In His arms, in His arms,
And no danger will I fear,
    In His arms, in His arms.

Here no storms can e'er molest,
    In His arms, in His arms,
Here the tired can find their rest
    In His arms, in His arms.

There's a haven for the lost,
    In His arms, in His arms,
From the wild waves where they tossed,
    In His arms, in His arms.

Chorus

See His loving arms outreaching,
    For you now, for you now
And His tender voice entreating,
    For you now, for you now.

THE DEAR LORD CHRIST

I want to serve, the dear Lord Christ,
    In a big strong noble way,
I wish to give, what days I live,
    In work that I know will pay.

I want to please, the dear Lord Christ,
    With the talents given me,
His message bring in songs I sing,
    That will bless humanity.

I want to love, the dear Lord Christ,
    And prove it to Him today,
I'll give my best, His promise test,
    And will follow Him always.

I want to give, the dear Lord Christ,
    All a love like His demands,
And fill the place, in life's hard race,
    With a heart that He commands.

Chorus

    Let us crown Him,
    Let us crown Him,
Let us crown Him Lord of all
If He is not Lord of all,
Then He is not Lord at all,
    Let us crown Him,
    Let us crown Him,
Let us crown Him Lord of all.

OUR AUTHORITY

Before our Lord ascended,
    And sat at God's right hand,
He gave the Great Commission,
    "Go preach in every land";
He promised to empower them,
    With might from heaven sent,
The Spirit to endue them,
    He came with that intent.

But now our Lord is seated,
    In power at God's right hand
And all His vast authority
    Is placed at our command;
None now our rights may challenge,
    The blessing that we claim
His finished work has purchased,
    We take them in His name.

Our Lord has Satan, conquered,
    His stronghold entered in,
And broken his dominion,
    Thank God, we're free from sin!
The long, long night is ended,
    And freedom's morn is here,
We sing our songs of triumph,
    Our hearts are free from fear.

Chorus

"For all authority
Has been given unto Me
In heaven and on earth,
And to you I give the right
To use My name and might,
In this long bitter fight,
    'Till I come."

WHEN I AM GONE

The sun will shine, the day decline,
    When I am gone, when I am gone,
The moon in splendor rise and set,
And me the world will soon forget,
    When I am gone, when I am gone.

The seasons come, the seasons go,
    When I am gone, when I am gone,
The blossoms on the hillside blow,
And all their gorgeous beauty show,
    When I am gone, when I am gone.

The children laughing on the street,
    When I am gone, when I am gone,
Will joyously each other meet,
And all their happy playmates greet,
    When I am gone, when I am gone.

The waters splashing down the hill,
    When I am gone, when I am gone,
That made my soul in childhood thrill,
Will turn the wheel down at the mill,
    When I am gone, when I am gone.

The birds will sing their mating song,
    When I am gone, when I am gone,
And build their nest in the oak tree strong,
Working and singing the whole day long,
    When I am gone, when I am gone.

Men will promise and women pray,
    When I am gone, when I am gone,
The serious work, the careless play,
The world move on from day to day,
    When I am gone, when I am gone.

The stars at night their vigil keep,
    When I am gone, when I am gone,
On in their giant orbits sweep,
Thru azure blue in silence deep,
    When I am gone, when I am gone.

Where will I go, when tides outflow,
    When I am gone, when I am gone,
And I my friends no longer know,
And leave all scenes of love below?
    When I am gone, when I am gone.

REMIND ME

When I would falter or stop on the way,
My heart lose courage and I fail to pray,
Remind me, dear Lord, of that cross on the hill
Of the Man who hung there, Love's mission to fill.

When I am tempted to forget my call,
Abandon my mission, forsake it all,
Remind me, dear Lord, of that cross on the hill,
Of the Man who hung there, Love's mission to fill.

When I am weary and worn by the fight,
The way grows lonely and dark is the night,
Remind me, dear Lord, of that cross on the hill,
Of the Man who hung there, Love's mission to fill.

When I am happy—forget the world's pain,
Wrapt up in my work, and struggle for gain,
Remind me, dear Lord, of that cross on the hill,
Of the Man who hung there, Love's mission to fill.

Chorus

Stir in my being a passion, dear Lord,
To fulfill Thy mission, herald thy Word,
'Til every nation shall hear the glad song,
Of His redemption—they've waited so long.

ABOUT THE AUTHOR

Dr. E. W. Kenyon (1867–1948) was born in Saratoga County, New York. At age nineteen, he preached his first sermon. He pastored several churches in New England and founded the Bethel Bible Institute in Spencer, Massachusetts. (The school later became the Providence Bible Institute when it was relocated to Providence, Rhode Island.) Kenyon served as an evangelist for over twenty years. In 1931, he became a pioneer in Christian radio on the Pacific Coast with his show *Kenyon's Church of the Air*, where he earned the moniker "The Faith Builder." He also began the New Covenant Baptist Church in Seattle, Washington. In addition to his pastoral and radio ministries, Kenyon wrote extensively. Among his books are *The Blood Covenant*, *In His Presence*, *Jesus the Healer*, *New Creation Realities*, and *Two Kinds of Righteousness*.